THE DIFFERENCE BETWEEN BOAZ AND HOSEA

By
Dr Elton Powell

DEDICATION PAGE

To my wife, (Dr Vicky), my mother (Bettie),
daughters, (Jasmine), (Mease & Jennifer Carroll),
(Zharia Noel), (Elizabeth T Powell), (Cameo McClain),
(Essence Moye Powell), (Moriah), (Amina), (Nevaeh),
women nationwide, but especially the Black woman—
who has loved fiercely, forgiven deeply, and waited
faithfully.

This is for you.

For every time you were told to "just wait on Boaz,"

but were never seen in the complexity of your
healing.

For the Ruths, loyal, wise, and steady.

For the Gomers wounded, wandering, and still
worthy.

For the women who carry both.

May you know that God sees you.

May you remember that His love never leaves you behind

And may this book be the beginning of your wholeness, not what you are waiting for.

With deep reverence and love

This book is born from the voices I have heard in our families, our communities, Bible studies, prayer meetings, and passing conversations.

It was born from the quiet ache in many Black women who have been told to "wait" without being seen, praised without being protected, or expected to heal while still bleeding.

My hope in these pages was not to retell ancient Bible stories or struggles out of the great trials of slavery, to remind the reader of the past for the sake of inspiration.

It was to pull them into the present—into our streets, our sanctuaries, our souls. Boaz and Hosea are more than historical men.

They are archetypes of two quite various kinds of love and two quite different types of assignments.

But this book is not about Boaz or Hosea.

It is about the Black woman who deserves to know that God is not punishing her through love.

He is preparing her through love—sometimes through peace, and sometimes through pain.

Whether you are in a Ruth season or a Gomer struggle, know this:

You are still in God's plan. And you are still worth choosing.

With gratitude,

+++Dr. Elton Powell

ACKNOWLEDGEMENT

With heartfelt thanks and deep gratitude, I want to express my appreciation to everyone who has supported my ministry and given me the opportunity to grow. Your prayers, encouragement, and belief in the calling upon my life have been a constant source of strength. Every word written in these pages has been shaped by your love, support, and faithfulness.

To Pastor Garland Jones of Mt. Zion Christian Church—thank you for the many conversations we've shared concerning Boaz. Those moments of dialogue, wisdom, and revelation have deeply influenced this work and expanded my spiritual understanding of purpose and divine connection.

To Daniel, along with the editors and graphic designers at American's Publisher, I offer my sincere appreciation for your excellence and professionalism. Your attention to detail, creative insight, and dedication helped perfect this book and bring its vision to life.

To Archbishop Lorenzo Peterson, thank you for giving me the opportunity to grow and serve in ministry. Your leadership and trust have been instrumental in my development. To Dr. Darryl T. Canady, thank you for training, inspiring, and equipping me for the work of ministry. Your teaching has challenged me to reach higher and serve with integrity and compassion.

To my mother, whose story of brokenness became a testimony of redemption—thank you for your faithfulness that led you to my father, the late Willie H.

Powell, your Boaz. Your journey has been a living example of the beauty of God's restoration and the power of unwavering faith.

To my dear and beautiful wife, Dr. Vicky Powell—your love has strengthened me emotionally, spiritually, and mentally. You have been my anchor, my confidant, and my encourager. Your unwavering support and belief in me gave me the courage and focus to complete this book.

And finally, to every woman who worked under my leadership at NEED, Inc. in Rocky Mount, North Carolina—thank you for your commitment, your faith, and your willingness to grow alongside me. Each of you has contributed to my journey in ways words cannot fully express.

To all who have supported me in any capacity—thank you. Your love, prayers, and faith have been the pillars that upheld this work. I pray that this book not only blesses you but also reminds you that every act of obedience, faith, and perseverance is never in vain.

With deepest gratitude,

Dr. Elton Powell

PICTURES GALLERY

TABLE OF CONTENTS

FOREWORD

The greatest gift my husband has given me in our years together is the insight to see the world not as a series of conflicts, but as a space where faith and intellect beautifully coexist. With his background as both an Archbishop and a high school science teacher, he has mastered the art of bridging the sacred and the secular.

His extensive academic background in Religion and Philosophy, culminating in a PhD, was never just an intellectual pursuit; it was a quest to understand the deeper truths that bind our universe. This book is the culmination of that quest. It tackles the intellectual and spiritual aspects of both Boaz and Hosea by showing how both spiritual and secular inquiry can lead to a more complete and profound understanding of the phrase, "I'm waiting for my Boaz.

The arguments you are about to read are not theoretical exercises. They are the product of 40 years of lived experience—in the parish, in the pulpit, and in the classroom. What you will discover within these pages is a roadmap for navigating some of life's most complex questions.

My husband's unique voice—wise, compassionate, and intellectually robust—will guide you toward a deeper truth. It is a powerful reminder that we can approach the great mysteries of our faith and the wonders of our world not with division, but with a sense of awe and harmony. I invite you to turn the page and join in on this remarkable journey.

The Scriptures of the Bible are filled with vivid characters whose lives serve as powerful parables for our own. In the Old Testament, few characters are as celebrated for their integrity and faith as Boaz, and few stories are as hauntingly beautiful and tragic as that of the prophet Hosea. At first glance, the two men appear to have little in common. One is the noble kinsman-redeemer of Ruth; a man of upright character who graciously accepts and provides for a foreigner in his land.

The other is a prophet commanded by God to marry a woman named Gomer, whose painful story of betrayal and redemption mirrors God's own relationship with His people.

Yet, in this groundbreaking book, my husband reveals that the most profound insights are often found not in obvious parallels, but in striking contrasts. "The Difference Between Boaz and Hosea" offers a breathtaking, 360-degree view of divine love—a love that encompasses both steadfast provision and relentless pursuit. Boaz represents the divine love that we understand and expect. He is the upright, respected man who provides security and legitimacy to the desolate.

His story is one of covenantal faithfulness and grace, portraying a patient, powerful love that restores and uplifts. In Boaz, we see a picture of redemption that is earned and deserved by the faithful, and his actions foreshadow the saving work of a future Messiah, Jesus Christ. But what of the love that goes beyond our expectations? This is the domain of Hosea. He is not a

2

redeemer sought by the faithful, but a devoted husband commanded to pursue the unfaithful.

His is a story of scandalous, humiliating, and persistent love that runs counter to all human instincts of pride and justice. Through his personal agony, Hosea gives us a glimpse into the heart of a God whose love is not based on merit, but on an unbreakable, undeserved commitment.

By placing these two figures side by side, this book challenges us to expand our understanding of God's nature. It forces us to ask critical questions: Do we prefer the tidy, respectable narrative of Boaz over the messy, painful story of Hosea? Can we accept a God who not only provides for the faithful, but also relentlessly pursues the unfaithful?

Ultimately, this book is more than a comparative study of two biblical figures. It is an exploration of the multi-faceted love of God, which is at once righteous and radical, but also predictable and surprising. The insights contained within these pages will provide a richer, more complete picture of God's redemptive plan and deepen our appreciation for the fullness of His grace. Prepare to have your understanding of divine love challenged and expanded.

Apostle Dr Vicky Powell

Co-Pastor of Nehemiah Wall Outreach Ministries

In a world where love and relationships are often reduced to fleeting emotion and quick satisfaction, The Difference Between Boaz and Hosea offers a powerful reminder of what true commitment, character, and divine purpose look like. Through the biblical lives of Boaz and Hosea, this book explores two very different stories of love one grounded in redemption and choice, the other in obedience and sacrifice. A thoughtful comparison of two righteous yet radically different men of the Bible, this work invites readers to reflect deeply on what kind of love story God may be writing in their own lives.

Boaz represents favor, provision, and timing, a man who chose Ruth not out of pity, but with clarity and purpose. Many of us have been taught to "wait for our Boaz," seeking a partner who will see our worth and redeem our past. But few have considered what it means to be loved like Gomer broken, unfaithful, yet still pursued relentlessly by a Hosea. Hosea, on the other hand, demonstrates a love that endures through heartbreak and rejection, reflecting God's unrelenting grace even in the face of betrayal.

This contrast challenges us not only to reflect on the kind of love we desire, but also on the kind of love we are called to give. Both men were obedient to God's will, but their journeys and the lessons they leave couldn't be more distinct.

The author of this work brings insight, wisdom, and compassion to every page. The author does not romanticize the pain or sugarcoat the truth. Instead, the author leads us into a deeper understanding of

God's heart and how the two men's love is often reflected in the complexity of human relationships.

Whether you are navigating your own season of waiting, healing from past hurt, or simply hungry for a richer spiritual perspective, The Difference Between Boaz and Hosea will speak to your soul. It is a timely, truthful guide for anyone seeking clarity in love and purpose in faith. This foreword cannot capture the full richness of what lies ahead in these pages. But I encourage you to read slowly, reflect honestly, and consider what season you're in: Are you waiting for a Boaz or walking through a Hosea experience? Either way, there is wisdom here for you.

Dr. Shiquita P. Blue

Co-Founder of Bountiful Achievement Resource Service, Inc.

CHAPTER 1:
"I'M WAITING ON MY BOAZ" – THE URBAN THEOLOGY

"I'm just waiting on my Boaz..."

A statement filled with longing, conviction, and hope for many women, especially African American women.

It is a phrase you have heard in churches, on social media, in girlfriend circles, or whispered in late-night prayers. "I'm waiting on my Boaz" is more than just a biblical reference. It has become a declaration of hope in the face of heartbreak, a prayer for protection after pain, and a cultural anthem for many Black women seeking love that feels safe, godly, and real.

But hidden beneath that phrase is a deeper question: Why Boaz and not Hosea? Why do women long for a Boaz, a man who recognized and married a noble, loyal woman named Ruth—but shy away from the painful, redemptive love story of Hosea, the prophet called to marry a promiscuous woman named Gomer?

The answer is layered. Boaz stands for provision, protection, honor, and legacy—qualities often absent in the historical treatment of African American women. He is safe. He is gentle. He is a provider. His story with Ruth offers a kind of fairy tale ending—rooted in respect and reward.

Hosea, however, is a different kind of love. One that bleeds. One that weeps. One that loves not for what it gains but for what it gives. Hosea's love was not romantic; it was obedient, prophetic, and painful. To many, Hosea's love feels too costly—too sacrificial—to be appealing. And Gomer? Her name carries the weight of shame. She is seen not as a hero, but as a harlot, not as a woman of virtue, but as a woman of damage.

Yet, both stories are essential. And both men—Boaz and Hosea—were used by God to display divine love.

The Cultural Weight Behind the Phrase

The popularity of "I'm waiting on my Boaz" reflects more than a desire for a godly husband. It reflects a deep, generational cry for healing, wholeness, and worth. For African American women—historically hyper-sexualized, dehumanized, and often expected to carry communities without support—the idea of Boaz is not just about romance. It is about restoration.

In a society that rarely celebrates Black women without conditions, Boaz is the one who will see her, choose her, and cover her—just as she is.

But this expectation, when misaligned, can become spiritualized fantasy. A fixation on Boaz can make us blind to the Hosea's in our lives—those who may be called to love us through our own healing. It may cause us to only desire love that feels good, rather than love that does good.

The Spiritual Implication

The "waiting" mindset can also quietly reinforce harmful theology. Many women internalize the idea that their worth is proven by being found, and that waiting is a passive act of worthiness. But Ruth was not just "waiting" for Boaz. She was working in the field. She was faithful to Naomi. She was courageous in a culture where widows were vulnerable. She was active in her obedience, and her reward came not from her perfection but from her posture of humility and action.

Boaz noticed Ruth because Ruth positioned herself— boldly and wisely—at his feet in a deeply symbolic gesture. She did not seduce; she gave. She did not chase; she chose to trust. And Boaz responded with honor.

Contrast this with Gomer, who ran from Hosea, who betrayed him, and who returned to her past and was enslaved by it. Yet even then, Hosea pursued her. He bought her back. He reclaimed her when society rejected her. His love cost him something public, personal, and prophetic.

Why the Church Has Preferred Boaz

Let us be honest. The Church, especially in Black communities, has often celebrated Ruth and Boaz as the gold standard. Women are urged to "wait for their Boaz" while being told, implicitly, not to be like Gomer. The message is clear: be the woman worth pursuing, not the woman needing rescue. Be virtuous. Be found. Be pure.

But this overlooks something radical: Gomer, the woman no one wanted, was still chosen—by God's command. And Hosea's love for her mirrored God's love for Israel, and for us. We are all Gomer. Broken. Betraying. In need of being bought back from the slavery of our sin.

To dismiss Gomer is to dismiss the gospel.

The Modern Reality

Today, many African American women find themselves somewhere between Ruth and Gomer. Some are loyal and steady, doing all the "right things," yet are overlooked. Others have known the street life, sexual trauma, abuse, or survival-driven choices that mirror Gomer's past. Yet all desire love. All deserve dignity. And all are seen by God. To pit Boaz and Hosea against each other is to misunderstand the point. God used both men to show two sides of divine love: Boaz shows that love honors; Hosea shows that love heals.

Both are needed. Both are sacred. And both are possible.

Chapter 2:
Biblical Background – Who Was Boaz?

Boaz is often remembered as the ideal man—strong, godly, generous, and honorable. But to understand the full weight of who Boaz was, we must strip away the romanticized lens and dig deeper into the historical, cultural, and theological context of his story. Boaz was not just a husband to Ruth—he was a relative redeemer, a man of character, and a prophetic figure in the lineage of Christ.

His story, found in the Book of Ruth, is one of compassion, providence, and redemption. But to appreciate Boaz, we must first understand the world in which he lived and the woman he chose.

A Man of Standing

Boaz is introduced in Ruth 2:1 as "a wealthy and influential man in Bethlehem." The Hebrew term used is Gibbor Chayil, which can be translated as "a man of valor" or "a mighty man of wealth." This title meant more than just financial prosperity—it conveyed that Boaz was a man of reputation, moral integrity, and social power. He was not merely rich; he was respected.

He owned fields during a time when land was one of the most valuable assets a man could have. He employed reapers, had influence over the community, and was known at the city gate, where legal and business matters were conducted. But what made Boaz stand out was not his status but his spirit.

The Time of the Judges

Boaz lived during the time of the judges, a lawless period marked by moral and spiritual decline in Israel. The final verse of Judges states, "In those days there was no king in Israel; everyone did what was right in his own eyes" (Judges 21:25). Against this backdrop of chaos and disobedience, Boaz's righteousness is revolutionary.

In a time when men exploited, degraded, and dishonored women, Boaz protected, respected, and elevated one. That was a radical act of obedience.

Ruth's Reputation, Boaz's Response

Ruth was a Moabite—a foreigner, an outsider. In Jewish tradition, the Moabites were a cursed people, born from an incestuous relationship between Lot and his daughter (Genesis 19:30–38). According to Deuteronomy 23:3, "No Ammonite or Moabite or any of their descendants may enter the assembly of the Lord, even down to the tenth generation."

And yet Ruth, a widowed Moabite woman, found favor in the eyes of Boaz. Why?

Because Boaz did not judge her by her past. He recognized her character, her loyalty to Naomi, and her faith in the God of Israel. In Ruth 2:11–12, Boaz says:

> "I have been told all about what you have done for your mother-in-law... how you left your father and mother and your homeland and came to live with a people you did not know before. May the Lord repay you for what you have done."

He blessed her, not based on bloodline, but based on obedience. He saw Ruth the way God sees us—not by where we come from, but by the steps of faith we take in the direction of redemption.

The Law of the Kinsman Redeemer

Boaz was more than just a good man—he was a Go'el, a relative redeemer. According to Levitical law (Leviticus 25:25, Deuteronomy 25:5–10), if a man died without children, his closest male relative had the responsibility to marry the widow and preserve the family line.

But here is what is profound: Boaz was not the closest relative. Another man had the legal right to marry Ruth, but he refused—because redeeming her meant redeeming her deceased husband's land, name, and lineage. It was a costly responsibility.

Boaz, knowing the full cost, willingly stepped in. He negotiated the legal terms at the city gate (Ruth 4), declared his intentions publicly, and married Ruth— not for personal gain, but for the sake of redemption.

He covered her. He restored her. He lifted her name and legacy out of obscurity and into history.

The Prophetic Lineage

Boaz and Ruth had a son named Obed. Obed fathered Jesse. Jesse fathered David. And from David came Jesus, the Messiah.

Think about that.

A Moabite widow and a man from Bethlehem birthed the bloodline of the King of Kings.

God chose a woman who was once an outcast to be the grandmother of King David. And He chose a man like Boaz—gentle, faithful, discerning—to help write that legacy.

Boaz was not just part of a love story. He was a shadow of Christ.

Jesus, too, is our relative redeemer. He, too, saw our unworthiness and loved us anyway. He, too, paid the price to bring us into the family of God. Boaz did not just redeem Ruth—he stood for the redeeming heart of God.

What Made Boaz Different?

In a culture where power was used to oppress, Boaz used his power to protect. In a society that overlooked women like Ruth, he looked closer. In a generation where everyone did what was right in their own eyes, Boaz did what was right in God's.

He was not drawn to Ruth because she was beautiful, seductive, or powerful. He was drawn to her because she was faithful, humble, and loyal.

He did not "rescue" her from her pain—he partnered with her in God's plan.

Boaz reminds us that godly love is not passive—it is protective. It does not exploit weakness—it covers it. It does not manipulate—it redeems.

The Boaz Ideal vs. Real-Life Relationships

Today, the idea of "Boaz" has become idealized—sometimes to the point of fantasy. But the real Boaz was not perfect—he was faithful. He was not rich in romance—he was rich in righteousness.

Many women pray for a Boaz but are often attracted to men who show none of his traits. The truth is that Boaz's qualities—integrity, patience, discernment, and spiritual maturity—often go unnoticed in a world that celebrates status over substance.

But if we are to genuinely want a Boaz, we must also be willing to wait like Ruth—working, trusting, submitting to God's timing, and staying faithful to the process of redemption.

CHAPTER 3:
BIBLICAL BACKGROUND – WHO WAS HOSEA?

Where Boaz's story is often quoted with admiration, Hosea's is whispered with discomfort. This is not the story you share at bridal showers or women's conferences. This is the story that hurts. That confuses. That offends the romantic sensibilities of the modern believer. And yet, Hosea's story is deeply prophetic, showcasing God's relentless, sacrificial, and sometimes scandalous love for His people.

Hosea was not a man most would choose as a relationship model. Not because he lacked character, but because he was called to carry heartbreak as ministry. He was a prophet of God during one of Israel's most corrupt and spiritually rebellious seasons. And what God asked of him was nothing short of shocking:

> "Go, marry a promiscuous woman and have children with her, for like an adulterous wife this land is guilty of unfaithfulness to the Lord."
>
> —Hosea 1:2 (NIV)

That woman's name was Gomer.

Hosea's Calling: A Prophetic Heartbreak

To understand Hosea's assignment, we must understand his context. Hosea prophesied to the northern kingdom of Israel during the reign of Jeroboam II, around the 8th century BCE. On the surface, it was a time of prosperity—military victories, territorial expansion, and economic growth. But spiritually, it was a time of idolatry, corruption, and betrayal of God's covenant.

The people worshiped Baal and other foreign gods. They practiced ritual prostitution. They violated justice. And worst of all, they abandoned the intimate relationship they once had with God.

In response, God did not just send Hosea to preach— He sent him to live out the message. Hosea's marriage would become a living, bleeding parable. His home would become a mirror of God's heart. His pain would become prophecy.

Gomer: The Woman No One Would Choose

We are introduced to Gomer not with her beauty, but with her shame. She is a woman known for promiscuity, involved in temple prostitution, which was common in pagan religious practices at the time. She is the antithesis of Ruth.

Where Ruth was noble, Gomer was notorious. Where Ruth clung, Gomer ran. Where Ruth's love story ended in security, Gomer's began in scandal.

And yet, God chose her—not because of her purity, but to display His power to redeem.

Hosea obeyed God's voice and married Gomer. They had children together—each with a symbolic name that reflected God's judgment on Israel:

Jezreel – meaning "God will sow," symbolizing the coming destruction.

Lo-Ruhamah – meaning "no mercy."

Lo-Ammi – meaning "not my people."

These names told Israel exactly how God felt about their betrayal. But behind the judgment was a brokenhearted love, a longing for reconciliation. Hosea's story was God's heart exposed.

The Pain of Unfaithfulness

Despite marrying Gomer, loving her, and fathering children with her, Hosea watched her walk away. She returned to her old ways. She gave herself to other lovers. She was not just unfaithful—she was enslaved by her past. Eventually, she was sold into bondage, either as a concubine, a prostitute, or a servant.

And here is where the story becomes stunning.

God told Hosea to go and buy her back.

"The Lord said to me, 'Go, show your love to your wife again, though she is loved by another man and is an adulterer. Love her as the Lord loves the Israelites.'"

—Hosea 3:1

Hosea found her. He paid a price. He brought her home. He did not shame her—he covered her. He did not discard her—he restored her.

And in doing so, he revealed a truth the world still struggles to grasp: real love is not rooted in worthiness—it is rooted in covenant.

Hosea's Love: A Mirror of God's Grace

Hosea's life was not romantic—it was redemptive. He loved a woman who did not know how to stay. He kept a covenant with someone who broke every rule. He stayed when others would have left. He paid for what already belonged to him.

Why?

Because Hosea's love was a mirror. A mirror of God's love for His people. A mirror of Christ's love for the church.

Israel had prostituted herself to idols. She was unfaithful. She broke the covenant. And yet, God was not finished with her. His mercy still reached. His love was still pursued.

And so did Hosea.

A Message to the Marginalized

Gomer's story is not just a tale of shame. It is a gospel invitation. It says to every woman who has ever been abandoned, abused, or addicted—you are not beyond redemption.

Gomer is the woman who has survived sexual exploitation.

Gomer is the woman who sold her body to feed her children.

Gomer is the woman who was molested as a child and confused love with pain.

Gomer is the woman who married for security, not love.

Gomer is the woman who goes to church on Sunday and dances at the club on Saturday, still searching for peace.

She has been mislabeled, misjudged, and misunderstood. But to God, she is redeemable.

And Hosea? He is the man who loves like Christ. He does not run from brokenness—he runs into it. He does not need perfection—he gives protection. Hosea's love is not the love of fairy tales—it is the love of faith.

Hosea vs. Boaz: Two Loves, One God

Boaz redeems a faithful woman.

Hosea redeems an unfaithful one.

Boaz operates within the law.

Hosea operates beyond it.

Boaz's story is neat, sweet, and satisfying.

Hosea's story is messy, painful, and powerful.

And yet, both are divine.

Boaz reveals the God who sees our virtue. Hosea reveals the God who sees our wounds.

God did not just call Hosea to love—He called him to suffer in love to reflect the heart of the divine. His story reminds us that true redemption is not always glamorous—but it is always glorious.

CHAPTER 4:
FROM SHACKLES TO SILENCE – THE JOURNEY OF THE AFRICAN AMERICAN WOMAN

The story of the African American woman is not just historical—it is biblical. It echoes through the lives of Ruth and Gomer. Her tears have watered generations. Her voice—though silenced—has prophesied through pain. She is the bruised backbone of a people, the often-forgotten heartbeat of both survival and spiritual resilience. From the cargo holds of slave ships to corporate boardrooms and corner churches, her journey is both sacred and scarred.

To understand why many African American women cry out, "I'm waiting for my Boaz," and yet live like Gomer, we must travel back—beyond emancipation, beyond cotton fields—to a place where identity, value, and womanhood were first stolen.

Shackled in Flesh, but Not in Faith

The transatlantic slave trade did not just chain bodies—it ripped apart families, erased names, redefined worth, and systematically dismantled the identity of the African woman. Stripped of language, culture, and protection, Black women were reduced to property—breeders, workers, and concubines.

They were raped without recourse, sold without consent, and forced to birth children they could not keep. Like Gomer, many were trapped in sexual cycles for survival—not by choice, but by cruel demand.

Enslaved women were forced into relationships that bore the illusion of marriage, but under the law, they were never truly wives—only bodies in bondage.

Yet, during dehumanization, they whispered prayers. They sang spirituals under moonlight. They nursed white children while mourning their own. Their resilience was not romantic—it was revolutionary.

The Silent Suffering

The post-slavery era brought no sudden healing. Jim Crow laws replaced shackles with segregation. Sharecropping became a new form of enslavement. Black women worked tirelessly as domestic housekeepers by day, church mothers on Sunday.

They bore the weight of racism and sexism simultaneously. Their silence was not consent—it was survival.

They were expected to be strong, even when dying inside. Expected to serve, even when starving. Expected to endure, even when empty.

They became the "mules of the world," as Zora Neale Hurston once said—carrying burdens no one else would acknowledge. They were Ruths in character, but often seen as Gomers in culture—objectified, overlooked, misunderstood.

Passion and Pain: The Sacred Duality

To be a Black woman in America is to live in constant contradiction. Loved yet unloved. Needed yet ignored. Feared yet desired.

Even in relationships, many are raised to be strong, independent, ambitious, and resilient. Yet beneath the strength is a deep longing to be covered. To be chosen. To be seen like Ruth was seen by Boaz—not just for beauty, but for integrity. Not just for what she offers, but for who she is.

Others have lived as Gomer—used, abandoned, or choosing transactional relationships out of necessity. Some have sold their bodies—not because they were unworthy, but because they were hungry. Bills needed to be paid. Children needed to eat. And slowly, survival became identity. Shame became normal. Pain became currency.

But here is the truth: God never defined them by their past. He still does not.

From Cotton Fields to Corporate America

Today's African American woman carries generations of unhealed wounds. She may wear designer clothes, hold degrees, and sit at boardroom tables, but often still battles internal wars—wars inherited through generational trauma and sustained by systemic oppression.

She is the first to rise and the last to rest.

She is the entrepreneur, the educator, the caretaker, the warrior.

She still often makes less money, works more hours, and raises children alone.

And in the church, she is the backbone—yet rarely the bride.

She serves faithfully, gives generously, and worships fiercely. But still, she hears the whispers: "Where is your Boaz?"

Gomer's Granddaughters: The Modern Struggle

Many modern women have Gomer's DNA—not in shame, but in struggle.

They want stability but have known only chaos.

They long for marriage but have only tasted misuse.

They look for covering but find criticism.

Some have turned to fast money, street life, or OnlyFans. Others hide their past under pristine appearances, afraid of being judged by the very community that should offer grace. And while some preach about Boaz, they forget that Ruth had to glean in the field, wait patiently, and make her intentions known in humility.

Likewise, they forget that Gomer did not find Hosea—Hosea found her when she was lost and broken.

Redeeming the Narrative

The African American woman's story is not simply a tale of survival—it is one of sacred redemption. She is not forgotten. She is not just "waiting for Boaz." She is becoming Ruth. She is being pursued like Gomer.

And she is being reminded that her worth is not found in her wounds.

As a community, we must do better. We must see our women not as statistics, but as sisters, not as problems to fix, but as people to honor. We must love them like Boaz—honorably like Hosea—sacrificially.

Because behind every "strong Black woman" is a little girl who wanted to be loved. Behind every Gomer is a woman who needs a Hosea. Behind every Ruth is a woman who needs a Boaz.

And behind every story is a Savior who still redeems.

CHAPTER 5:
BECOMING RUTH – THE HEART OF A REDEEMABLE WOMAN

"I'm waiting for my Boaz" is more than a phrase—it is a declaration of hope, a badge of faith, a whispered desire that in a world full of Gomers, Boaz is still possible. But rarely do we stop to ask, what kind of woman attracts a Boaz? Who was Ruth? What set her apart? And what can her story teach the modern woman, especially the African American woman who has been told to survive more than she has been taught to thrive?

This chapter turns our gaze from pain to purpose, from the scars of Gomer to the strength of Ruth. Ruth was not born in privilege. She was not flawless. But she was faithful. And that faithfulness positioned her for favor.

Let us explore her legacy.

A Widow with Nothing but Integrity

Ruth was a Moabite—a woman from a nation despised by Israel. She married into an Israelite family who had left Bethlehem during a famine. Her husband died. Her brother-in-law died. Her father-in-law died. She was left with nothing but a grieving mother-in-law, Naomi, and a decision: return to her homeland or walk into the unknown with Naomi's God.

She chose covenant.

"But Ruth replied, 'Do not urge me to leave you or to turn back from you. Where you go, I will go, and where you stay, I will stay. Your people will be my people and your God my God.'"

—Ruth 1:16 (NIV)

In this one verse, we see the first marker of a Ruth: loyalty rooted in love, not convenience.

Ruth could have gone back to comfort, to culture, to the familiar. Instead, she chose obedience, humility, and selflessness.

Ruth's Character: Qualities That Still Speak

Loyalty That Defies Logic

She stayed with Naomi when others left. This was not about companionship—it was about covenant. Ruth understood that sometimes, love means choosing the harder road. Loyalty is not about who deserves it—it is about who you decide to honor.

In a culture of disposable relationships, loyalty is radical.

Humility in Action

When they arrived in Bethlehem, Ruth did not expect handouts. She got to work—gleaning in the fields, risking danger, doing the work others ignored.

She was not too proud to labor. She did not demand Boaz's attention—she proved her character. Before Ruth got Boaz's favor, she earned his respect.

In today's world, this speaks volumes. Ruth teaches us that favor follows faithfulness, not fame.

Initiative Without Manipulation

Ruth did not chase Boaz—but she did not hide from him either. Under Naomi's guidance, she positioned herself with dignity and clarity. Her actions at the threshing floor (Ruth 3) were not seductive—they were symbolic. She uncovered his feet as a cultural request for covering, not to stir lust.

In a generation taught to "make the first move" or "play hard to get," Ruth teaches balance—be seen without being loud; be present without being desperate.

Faith That Transcends Background

Ruth was not born into Israel's covenant—she chose it. She broke away from generational patterns. She turned her back on idol worship and pursued a God she did not fully understand. Her past did not limit her—her faith liberated her.

For many African American women navigating their worth, their past, and their pursuit of love, Ruth reminds us: you are not where you came from. You are what you commit to becoming.

Ruth and the Modern Woman

Many women today feel torn between being a Ruth and surviving like Gomer. Some ask, Can I really become a Ruth after living like Gomer? The answer is yes. The journey to Boaz is not about being perfect—it is about being positioned.

Ruth did not come with money.

She did not come with prestige.

She came with obedience, humility, and faith.

And Boaz—a wealthy, godly man—not only noticed her, but he also redeemed her. Not because she demanded it, but because she showed who she was.

The Black Ruth: A Hidden Legacy

The African American woman has often lived with Ruth's heart and Gomer's reality. She has been faithful in silence. She has worked two jobs and raised three children. She is tithed, served, and prayed for a husband while watching others get chosen first.

She has been Naomi's caregiver, Ruth's worker, and Gomer's victim—all in one body.

But hear this: your Ruth-ness is not erased by your Gomer history.

You may have been mistreated.

You may have been misunderstood.

You may have made mistakes.

But if you are walking in faith, you are walking in Ruth's legacy.

Ruth's Reward

Ruth's story ends not just in romance—but in redemption. Boaz marries her, not out of pity, but out of honor. He sees her. He covers her. He protects her.

And together, they birth Obed—father of Jesse, father of David—the line of Jesus Christ.

From a Moabite widow to the great-great-grandmother of the Messiah.

Her faithfulness became her legacy. And yours can too.

Becoming Ruth

You do not become Ruth by mimicking her culture—you become Ruth by mirroring her character.

Stay loyal when it is easier to leave.

Work humbly when no one applauds.

Position yourself with wisdom, not seduction.

Choose covenant, not convenience.

Let your past be a testimony, not a title.

You do not wait for Boaz; you become the woman. Boaz is praying for.

CHAPTER 6:
HOSEA AND GOMER – A SCANDALOUS LOVE REDEEMED BY GOD

Most love stories begin with attraction. This one begins with a command.

> "The Lord said to Hosea, 'Go, marry a promiscuous woman and have children with her, for like an adulterous wife this land is guilty of unfaithfulness to the Lord.'"
>
> —Hosea 1:2 (NIV)

It is a shocking assignment. God does not suggest. He instructs. He tells Hosea, a prophet, to marry a woman who will not be faithful. A woman known not for her virtue but her vice. A woman like Gomer.

This is not the story we tell in women's conferences. We talk about Esther's crown, Ruth's harvest, and Mary's womb. But Gomer? She is the woman we overlook—the woman we judge.

Yet God centered an entire prophetic book around her. Why?

Because her redemption is a mirror of ours.

Gomer: A Name, A Life, A Symbol

Gomer's name in Hebrew means "complete" or "to bring to an end." Ironically, her life seemed anything but whole. She is introduced not with a father's covering or a virtuous reputation, but with a title of shame: "a wife of whoredom."

She was not hidden in her struggle. Her brokenness was public. She is the woman many whisper about, but few weep for.

She may have been a prostitute before the marriage. Some scholars believe she returned to prostitution after marrying Hosea. Either way, her pattern of unfaithfulness was known to God—yet He still instructed Hosea to love her.

Why?

Because her story was bigger than her sin.

Hosea: The Prophet Who Loved Beyond Pain

Hosea was not a fool. He was a man of God—called to speak truth to a rebellious nation. His life became a living prophecy. His heartbreak became a divine metaphor.

God used Hosea's love for Gomer to reveal His own heart for Israel, a people who constantly abandoned Him for idols, but whom He refused to give up on.

This is divine love in dirty places.

Imagine Hosea standing in the town square, asking for his wife, who has returned to a life of whoredom. Imagine the stares, the scoffs, the humiliation.

Yet he searched for her.

He pursued her.

He bought her back.

"So, I bought her for fifteen shekels of silver and about a homer and a lethek of barley."

—Hosea 3:2 (NIV)

She belonged to him by covenant, but he still paid to redeem her.

Let that sink in.

Gomer's Redemption: A Picture of Grace

Gomer was not chased down because she changed. She was pursued while still broken. She was loved before she repented. She was rescued not because she earned it, but because Hosea was faithful.

This is not just romance—this is revelation.

Gomer's journey is symbolic of Israel's unfaithfulness, but also of our own. Her rescue is symbolic of Christ's redemption.

In many ways, Gomer is every woman who has ever:

Traded her worth for attention

Settled for survival instead of wholeness

Returned to what God called her out of

Been defined by her mistakes

Yet God says: You are still Mine.

The Modern Gomer: Still Pursued

There are countless modern-day Gomers—women who have lived through trauma, exploitation, and cycles of pain. Some were abused as children and never learned healthy love. Others were molested, silenced, or objectified before they even knew how to spell "dignity."

Some turned to fast money—selling their bodies in clubs, hotels, or behind screens. Some did not sell anything but gave everything—hoping love would buy commitment.

Their stories are rarely told in Sunday school. But their prayers? Heaven hears them loud.

Many want a Boaz but feel like Gomer. They believe Boaz is for the pure and pretty. They forget that Hosea—like Boaz—was a redeemer.

And even more so, they forget that Jesus—the ultimate Bridegroom—chooses the broken, the bruised, and the bound. He chooses them.

What Gomer Needed (and What Many Women Still Do)

Gomer did not just need rescue—she needed restoration. She needed:

Love that does not require performance

Hosea loved her before she got herself together. Just like God loves us.

A place to come home to

Gomer wandered. But when Hosea brought her back, he told her, "You must dwell with me." (Hosea 3:3)

He did not just reclaim her—he reintegrated her.

A new identity

We do not know Gomer's story after Hosea redeems her. The Bible goes silent. But that is the point: her story does not end in shame—it ends in silence because the work of grace had already spoken.

When Gomer Desires Boaz

Some women today carry Gomer's past but long for Boaz's presence. The tension is real. Can a woman once enslaved by addiction, lust, or pain be loved by a man of honor? Yes.

But first, she must know she has already been chosen by God.

The path from Gomer to Ruth is not linear—but it is possible. Redemption is not earned. It is received.

Once she embraces her identity in God, she no longer begs for Boaz—she attracts him. Because she walks in wholeness, not hiding.

Hosea's Heart: A Reflection for Men

Men, take note. Hosea teaches us that love is not always easy. It is not always convenient. But when led by God, it is transformative.

If God trusted Hosea to love a woman with a complicated past, what does that say about how He wants His sons to see His daughters today?

It says: Do not just chase beauty. Cover brokenness. Do not just seek perfection. Pursue purpose.

A Scandalous Love Redeemed

Hosea and Gomer's story is not neat. It is not sweet. It is raw. It is redemptive. It is the story of a God who will not stop loving people who keep leaving Him. It is the story of women who have been discarded by society but desired by heaven.

It is not a fairytale. It is better. Because it is true.

And it is still being written—in every woman who dares to believe that her past does not disqualify her from love, favor, or a future.

CHAPTER 7:
GOMER'S DAUGHTERS – WHEN LOVE FINDS YOU IN THE BROKEN PLACES

There is a quiet army of women who walk among us every day.

You see them at the bus stop. At the clinic. In the church pew. Behind the pulpit. On social media with filters and flawless makeup. But behind the image are stories too heavy for hashtags.

These are Gomer's daughters.

They are the women whose bodies have been used, whose names have been slandered, whose pasts have been monetized, and whose pain has been normalized. Some were trafficked. Some were abused. Some made choices to survive. Others were never given a choice at all.

And yet—they are still worthy of love.

Who Are Gomer's Daughters?

Gomer's daughters are not defined by biology—they are defined by experience. They are the women who:

Grew up in households without affection

We were molested by relatives and told to keep quiet

They were given attention only when they performed sexually

Learned to sell their worth to meet basic needs

Struggled to connect love with anything outside of pain

They learned survival. Not tenderness.

They learned performance. Not intimacy.

And somewhere along the way, they stopped believing that real love—even divine love—was possible.

But just like Gomer, they were never out of God's reach.

The Economic Exploitation of Black Women: A Historic Wound

To understand the plight of Gomer's daughters—especially within the African American community—we must go back.

During slavery, Black women were treated as property, bred like animals, and sexually exploited without justice. The auction block was not just for labor—it was for lust. Mothers were raped while their children watched. Wives were sold away from their husbands. Girls were forced into "favor" with slave owners just to be fed.

This historical trauma birthed a generational struggle with identity, sexuality, and self-worth.

Post-slavery did not bring healing—it brought Jim Crow, mass incarceration, and welfare policies that often displaced the Black male figure from the home, leaving women to bear it all.

So, when a Black woman today says, "I'm just trying to survive," she is speaking from generations of pain.

She is Gomer's daughter with Harriet's strength and Ruth's faith, walking through a world that still questions her value.

Survival Turned Struggle

Many women did not choose prostitution or promiscuity. They chose food. Rent. Protection. A way out.

And once survival turns into a pattern, shame sets in. By the time some women realize how far they have fallen, they no longer believe they are worthy of more.

But God still sees.

Just as Hosea went looking for Gomer in the marketplace, God sends prophets, counselors, pastors, and sometimes strangers to remind Gomer's daughters: You are more than your pain.

When Love Finds You There

Love does not wait for you to be perfect. Love finds you in the dirt.

It found the woman caught in adultery (John 8).

It found the Samaritan woman with five husbands (John 4).

It found Mary Magdalene, tormented by demons and judged by her past (Luke 8:2).

Each of these women could have been called "Gomer" by society. But Jesus never flinched. He called them daughter. Worthy. Redeemed.

And if He did it for them, He can do it for every woman reading this who feels disqualified by her yesterday.

The Challenge of Receiving Love After Trauma

For many Gomer's daughters, love is terrifying.

It is easier to be hurt than to be healed. Hurt is familiar. Healing is foreign. Trusting someone to love you unconditionally after years of conditional pain is not easy.

This is where therapy, community, and spiritual mentorship matter.

Love is not just emotional—it is reconstructive.

Gomer did not just need a home—she needed a heart overhaul. Many women today are the same. They need a safe space to learn how to be loved again. To trust. To breathe. To believe.

And yes—Boaz can love a former Gomer. But more importantly, she must first believe she is worthy of being loved.

A Letter to Gomer's Daughters

To the woman who gave her body to survive...

To the girl who was touched before she had a voice...

To the sister who dances in clubs but weeps in silence...

To the leader who preaches while hiding her past...

You are seen.

You are not disposable.

You are not dirty.

You are not beyond redemption.

There is nothing you have done that can outrun God's mercy.

The God who told Hosea to marry Gomer is the same God who says, "I have loved you with an everlasting love." (Jeremiah 31:3)

Let that love in. Not the love that manipulates. Not the lust that devours. But the love that restores.

You do not have to be perfect to be chosen.

You just must be willing to be found.

Gomer's Daughters Have Purpose

This world may try to label you, limit you, and shame you.

But Gomer's daughters are rising.

They are pastors and authors.

They are advocates and artists.

They are mothers and healers.

They are women who once bled in silence and now roar in purpose.

They may still carry scars—but those scars have turned into testimonies.

Your story is not over. It is only beginning.

CHAPTER 8:

BRUISED BUT BREATHING – THE CRY OF THE BLACK WOMAN FROM BONDAGE TO BECOMING

She is the mother and the martyr, the backbone and the broken. She is the cradle of life and the carrier of trauma. She is the rhythm of a people and the silence of centuries.

She is a Black woman.

She walks through America with the weight of history on her shoulders and the future in her womb. She has been beaten but not buried, overlooked but never obsolete. Her story is one of contradiction—bruised but breathing.

And like Gomer, she knows what it means to be used... yet still needed.

From Chains to Choices: A Historical Journey

The legacy of the African American woman in this nation is not a side note—it is a central narrative.

From the moment she was ripped from African soil and sold into slavery, she was stripped of her identity and reduced to utility. Her body was not her own. It was used to birth more slaves, to satisfy her oppressor's lust, to cook, clean, nurse, and be invisible all at once.

Unlike Ruth, who followed Naomi by choice, the Black woman followed captivity. Unlike Gomer, who returned to promiscuity out of brokenness, the Black woman was often forced into it by systemic design.

She was whipped for rebellion.

She was raped without consequence.

She was silenced by law.

She was stripped of dignity.

Yet, she endured.

Exploited, Then Erased

After Emancipation, freedom was promised but never fully delivered. The Reconstruction era introduced new chains—Jim Crow laws, lynching, voter suppression, and sexual coercion in domestic work.

Many Black women found themselves as maids in homes where they were still treated like property. They cooked the meals, cleaned the floors, and raised white children while being denied humanity.

Some turned to the only resource they had left—their bodies.

It was not a choice of desire, but of desperation. In urban cities and Southern towns, survival sex became currency. And once survival becomes your story, shame is a lifelong residue.

This pain is inherited. It is passed down through looks, phrases, fears, and instincts. It teaches daughters how to bend but not break. It teaches them to fight, but also to fear.

The Complexities of Survival

In modern America, the Black woman still bears disproportionate burdens:

She is more likely to be the head of household, balancing motherhood, career, and care for extended family—often without support.

She is more likely to experience poverty, despite being the most educated demographic in the U.S.

She is more likely to be incarcerated, trafficked, and misdiagnosed when it comes to mental health.

And yet, she still praises.

She still serves.

She still hopes for Boaz.

But sometimes, Boaz never shows up.

Instead, she becomes both Ruth and Boaz—harvesting in her own field, protecting her own children, praying over her own pain.

Sexuality, Silence, and the Church

One of the most complex realities for the Black woman is how her sexuality has been both weaponized and silenced.

In church, she is often told to cover up and be virtuous, but rarely is she asked how her sense of worth was formed. Few dare to ask:

Who taught her what love looks like?

What does she believe about her own body?

Has anyone ever told her her body is holy—even if it has been touched in unholy ways?

There are Gomers sitting in pews every Sunday, hiding under hats, wigs, and scriptures. They are tired of pretending. They long for a gospel that does not just save souls but heals stories.

They do not need condemnation—they need compassion.

They do not need silence—they need safe spaces.

The Black Woman's Cry: "Am I Still Worthy?"

In the quiet of the night, many Black women whisper questions that echo centuries:

Will I ever be chosen?

Am I too broken to be loved?

Can a man see me and not just use me?

Will God heal what history has broken?

These questions are sacred. They are not signs of weakness, but of deep, honest longing.

And here is the answer of God:

"You are altogether beautiful, my darling; there is no flaw in you."

Song of Songs 4:7 (NIV)

He sees you—not the residue of rape, not the echo of abandonment, not the trauma of survival. He sees you. He made in Genesis—before chains, before shame.

From Bondage to Becoming

The journey from bondage to becoming is not a straight line. It is a winding path of grief and glory.

But here is what we know:

Ruth found favor in a foreign land.

Gomer found redemption after ruin.

Tamar found justice after the assault.

Mary found purpose after the scandal.

The woman with the issue of blood found healing after years of isolation.

And so can the Black woman today.

She may not always feel like Ruth, but she can still reap. She may relate more to Gomer, but she can still be redeemed. She may feel more like Hagar—used and dismissed—but she must remember: God still sees (Genesis 16:13).

You Are Still Becoming

Dear sister, you are not your pain. You are not your past. You are not your poverty.

You reflect divine strength clothed in melanin.

Your hips carry the rhythm of nations. Your voice echoes prophets. Your womb cradles nations. Your soul is not for sale.

You are not just a survivor—you are a sign.

A sign that God can take the least likely and lift her up.

A sign that Gomer can be loved.

That Ruth still dwells among us.

That Boaz may yet come.

And that Jesus always will.

Chapter 9:
Ruth's Anointing – When Purpose and Position Meet

There is a sacred beauty in Ruth's story—one that transcends centuries and speaks into the soul of every woman who has ever lost something and dared to believe again.

Ruth was not born into privilege.

She was not born into the covenant.

She was not even born into the faith.

But she walked into her promise.

While many romanticize Ruth as the quiet woman who waited for Boaz, the truth is: Ruth did not wait—she worked, she followed, and she believed.

Her story is one of intentional movement and anointed obedience.

Ruth's anointing was not just in her beauty or humility—it was in her posture, her purpose, and her positioning.

Ruth Was Not a Woman of Perfection—She Was a Woman of Purpose

Many women today believe they must be perfect before they are positioned for love, destiny, or divine favor.

But Ruth's story tells another truth.

She was:

A Moabite, born to a nation birthed in incest (Genesis 19)

A widow, who had experienced death and loss

A foreigner, seen as an outsider in Bethlehem

A worker, laboring in the field just to eat

And yet—God saw fit to include her in the lineage of Jesus Christ (Matthew 1:5).

This is the power of Ruth's anointing: She turned what she was not into who she became 7 Traits of a Modern-Day Ruth

If you are a woman searching for your identity in a world full of Gomer-like expectations and Boaz-like hopes, Ruth offers a clear blueprint for sacred womanhood. Here are seven defining traits of Ruth's anointing:

1. Loyalty Without Limits

> "Where you go, I will go, and where you stay, I will stay." (Ruth 1:16)

Ruth did not just follow Naomi—she cleaved to her. She understood the covenant. Loyalty was not based on benefit; it was rooted in love.

Today's Ruth knows how to commit—even in dry seasons.

2. Humility in the Harvest

"Let me go to the fields and pick up the leftover grain..." (Ruth 2:2)

Ruth was not afraid of arduous work. She did not expect handouts. She gathered leftovers with grace until favor found her.

Humility will open doors that beauty never can.

3. Submission Without Shame

"She lay at his feet..." (Ruth 3:7)

In today's world, submission is seen as weakness. But Ruth's posture at Boaz's feet was a symbol of surrender—not subjugation. She trusted the process and honored the order.

True submission is strength in divine alignment.

4. Wisdom to Follow Divine Counsel

"Do whatever he tells you to do..." (Ruth 3:5)

Ruth did not just listen to Naomi—she obeyed. She recognized the wisdom in a seasoned woman. Modern Ruths value mentorship and do not confuse independence with rebellion.

5. Faith Over Familiarity

Ruth left her homeland, her culture, her gods, and her comfort. She chose faith over familiarity. That kind of courage is not accidental—it is anointed.

6. Grace Under Pressure

She worked among strangers. She lived on scraps. She loved despite loss. Ruth carried grace like a fragrance—it followed her into the field and into Boaz's heart.

7. Purpose Over Popularity

While others chased attention, Ruth chased purpose. She was not flashy—she was faithful. She did not need to be seen; she needed to be sent.

And God sent her into destiny.

Ruth's Positioning Was Not Random—It Was Prophetic

When Ruth "happened" to glean in Boaz's field (Ruth 2:3), it was not luck—it was alignment.

Sometimes what looks like a coincidence is a divine convergence.

Ruth was in the right field at the right time with the right heart.

She did not manipulate the moment—she ministered in it.

If you are a woman in a season of uncertainty, wondering if God has forgotten you—take heart in Ruth's positioning.

Your purpose may not look glorious yet, but God sees your field work.

Ruth's Heart Made Room for Boaz

did n

Women who carry Ruth's anointing do not have to chase Boaz.

They do not have to convince him.

They do not have to seduce him.

They simply become—and Boaz will recognize.

There Are Still Ruths Among Us

The world may be loud with Gomer's cry, but Ruth still lives—in the woman who:

Chooses healing over hiding

Works when others weep

Prays when others play

Believes that when others are bitter

She may be raising children alone. She may be taking night classes. She may be celibate in a sexual culture. She may be overlooked, underestimated, and underpaid.

But she carries the crown of purpose on her head and the cloak of grace on her shoulders.

She is not forgotten—she is being formed.

Ruth's Anointing Is Not Just for Marriage—It is for Ministry

While Ruth's story is often framed around romance, the deeper truth is that her life was prophetic. Her union with Boaz produced Obed... who fathered Jesse... who fathered David... who preceded Jesus.

Her legacy was not in her beauty—it was in her obedience.

You may not see the full fruit of your faith today— but every step you take in alignment with God is birthing something eternal.

CHAPTER 10:
HOSEA'S HEART – LOVING THE UNLOVABLE

If Ruth's story teaches us about faithfulness and favor, Hosea's story teaches us about sacrificial love and redemptive suffering. Hosea's journey is one of pain wrapped in purpose—a love so costly that it mirrors God's own love for His people.

When God told Hosea to marry Gomer, a woman described as promiscuous, He was asking more than obedience—He was calling Hosea to live a prophetic parable of grace.

The Call to Love the Unlovable

Hosea's marriage was no romantic fairy tale.

He was commanded to marry a woman who was unfaithful and whose lifestyle would bring public shame.

Imagine the emotional toll:

• Loving a spouse who is constantly leaving

• Bearing children who symbolize betrayal (names like Lo-Ruhamah, meaning "no mercy")

• Facing rejection and heartbreak repeatedly

Yet, Hosea said yes.

His obedience was a painful obedience, but a necessary one.

Why Did God Choose Hosea for This Mission?

Hosea's life was not simply a personal trial—it was a divine metaphor.

God used Hosea's painful marriage to symbolize His relationship with Israel, a people who repeatedly turned away, worshipping idols and breaking the covenant.

Just as Gomer was unfaithful to Hosea, Israel was unfaithful to God.

Yet, just as Hosea kept pursuing Gomer, God never stopped pursuing His people.

Hosea's Love Was Unconditional and Unyielding

Unlike Boaz, whose love was tender and protective, Hosea's love was raw and relentless.

Boaz loved Ruth as a reward for her faithfulness.

Hosea loved Gomer despite her unfaithfulness.

Boaz's love restored dignity.

Hosea's love demanded endurance.

What Can We Learn from Hosea's Example?

Hosea's story challenges us to rethink love—not as a feeling or a reward but as a commitment.

For African American women—many of whom carry the "Gomer DNA" of survival, pain, and brokenness—Hosea's love is a blueprint of grace.

It says:

- I will love you even when you do not love yourself.

- I will stand with you when others walk away.

- I will pursue you when you run.

- I will see beyond your mistakes to the child of God within.

Women with Gomer DNA Today

Many Black women carry scars of abandonment, addiction, abuse, and betrayal. These are their Gomer moments.

They may struggle with:

- Feeling unworthy of love

- Questioning if they can ever be redeemed

- Wrestling with cycles of hurt that seem impossible to break

Yet, Hosea's love teaches that no one is beyond hope.

Redemption is available—even for those who have fallen hardest.

Hosea's Love Points to Christ

Hosea's story is not just about one man and one woman—it is about the heart of God displayed through Jesus Christ.

Jesus is the ultimate Boaz and Hosea—redeeming, loving, restoring, and never giving up.

He embraces the Ruth and the Gomer in all of us.

His love is costly but unwavering.

The Strength It Takes to Love Like Hosea

Loving the unlovable requires:

- Patience: Waiting and hoping even when love is rejected

- Forgiveness: Choosing to forgive repeatedly without bitterness

- Faith: Trusting that love has the power to heal and transform

- Sacrifice: Putting another's healing and wholeness above personal comfort

The Beauty in Hosea's Pain

Though Hosea's path was filled with heartbreak, it produced fruit.

His marriage was a message of hope.

His story reminds us that sometimes love is not about what we get, but what we give—even when it hurts.

CHAPTER 11:
THE INTERSECTION OF BOAZ AND HOSEA IN THE BLACK WOMAN'S LIFE

In the tapestry of African American womanhood, the stories of Boaz and Hosea do not stand separately—they weave together into a complex pattern of love, pain, struggle, and redemption. Understanding these two men helps us grasp the full spectrum of relationships and healing that many Black women experience.

Two Models of Love, One Purpose

Boaz represents the rewarded love—the man who sees worth, honors loyalty, and restores dignity. Hosea represents the relentless love—the man who loves through brokenness, forgives unfaithfulness, and pursues even when it hurts.

Together, they reflect God's love in two powerful ways:

The love that protects and provides

The love that pursues and redeems

African American women often live at this intersection, seeking the tenderness of Boaz while wrestling with the reality of Hosea's sacrificial love.

The Reality of Black Women's Relationships

Historically, Black women have navigated relationships shadowed by slavery, systemic racism, economic oppression, and sexual exploitation. These conditions shaped a complex emotional landscape:

The Boaz desire: For a partner who respects, values, and cherishes them

The Hosea reality: Meeting men who may be broken themselves or facing the pain of unfaithfulness and neglect

This duality often leaves Black women caught between hope and hurt.

Why Both Are Necessary

Some may question why Black women would need to embrace both stories. The answer lies in wholeness.

The Boaz model offers restoration—a picture of love that uplifts and honors.

The Hosea model offers redemption—a pathway to healing through pain and forgiveness.

Neither story alone is sufficient to capture the breadth of love Black women deserve or endure.

Healing at the Crossroads

At the crossroads of Boaz and Hosea, African American women find:

The grace to wait for a love that honors their worth

The strength to forgive wounds inflicted by broken relationships

The courage to seek healing from trauma and cycles of abuse

The wisdom to discern when to stay and when to walk away

This is a complex journey—one that demands emotional resilience and spiritual depth.

Embracing the Boaz and Hosea Within

The stories also speak internally.

Every Black woman carries a bit of Ruth's loyalty and faithfulness.

Every Black woman also carries Gomer's scars and survival.

The internal Boaz is the voice that affirms, "You are worthy."

The internal Hosea is the voice that says, "I will love you through your brokenness."

Healing begins when these voices align, not in contradiction, but in harmony.

Moving Forward with Hope

The legacy of slavery and systemic oppression has tried to define Black women by their pain.

But Boaz and Hosea's stories say:

You are more than your struggles.

Your past does not dictate your future.

Love can be both tender and tenacious.

You are worthy of a love that restores and redeems.

Practical Steps for Healing and Growth

Cultivate Self-Worth: Believe you are valuable and deserving of respect.

Seek Healthy Relationships: Look for partners who show both Boaz-like respect and Hosea-like grace.

Embrace Spiritual Growth: Allow God's love to heal your wounds and empower your heart.

Build Support Networks: Surround yourself with community, mentors, and sisterhood.

Forgive but Set Boundaries: Learn when to forgive and when to protect yourself.

Own Your Story: Use your journey to empower others and create a legacy.

The intersection of Boaz and Hosea in the lives of African American women is a sacred space of challenge and hope.

It invites women to dream of Boaz's gentle provision while enduring Hosea's relentless love.

It is a call to rise from pain, reclaim identity, and embrace a future filled with divine love.

CHAPTER 12:
RUTH'S BOLDNESS: A BLUEPRINT FOR RECLAIMING AGENCY

In modern church circles, Ruth is often painted as the perfect, passive woman—quiet, obedient, and waiting for her man. But a closer reading of Scripture tells a much bolder story. Ruth was not timid. She was not just "waiting." She was strategic, brave, and spirit-led. She took a risk that changed not only her life but the lineage of King David and eventually Jesus Christ Himself.

This chapter is a reclamation of Ruth's boldness—not as seduction, but as godly agency. It is also a call for African American women to reclaim their own voice and agency in a world that has long tried to silence or distort it.

Ruth's Bold Move: Lying at the Feet of Redemption

When Ruth lay at Boaz's feet on the threshing floor, it was not a sexual overture—it was a radical act of covenant and courage. Ruth followed Naomi's direction, but she did so with wisdom, purity, and purpose.

She knew what she was doing.

She understood the Levirate tradition. She positioned herself not to manipulate, but to align with divine provision. Ruth was saying, "I am not waiting in the background hoping to be noticed. I know who I am. I know who you are. Let us do this God's way."

Too often, women are told to "just wait." But waiting without wisdom can lead to missed purpose.

The Silencing of Black Women's Boldness

Throughout history, African American women have been punished for being bold:

In slavery, boldness meant punishment—or death.

In the Jim Crow era, boldness was labeled as "attitude" or "insubordination."

In modern society, bold Black women are called "too loud," "too independent," or "too much."

But boldness, when rooted in purpose and faith, is not rebellion. It is reclamation. Ruth teaches us that holy boldness opens doors, shifts destinies, and positions you for favor.

Reframing Boldness in Today's World

Being bold today means:

Leaving abusive or dead-end relationships.

Going back to school after years of putting others first.

Starting that business even when the odds are stacked.

Advocating for your children, your health, and your healing.

Ruth's story reminds us that it is not about being perfect—it is about being positioned. Positioning yourself in humility and in courage.

Ruth Was a Risk Taker—And So Are You

The threshing floor is not just a physical place. It is a spiritual metaphor.

It is the place of separation, purification, and decision.

Many women today are at their own threshing floor moment:

Do I stay or go?

Do I hide or step forward?

Do I settle or speak up?

Like Ruth, you may not have wealth, connections, or guarantees—but you have faith, dignity, and divine timing. And that is more than enough.

God Honors Holy Boldness

God did not rebuke Ruth for her actions.

Boaz did not shame her.

He blessed her.

Why? Because her boldness was backed by character and covenant.

She was not chasing a man. She was walking with purpose.

Today, God still honors bold women who move in faith, obedience, and clarity.

CHAPTER 13:
THE SILENT PAIN OF GOMER – WHEN THE PAST STILL HAUNTS THE PRESENT

We often read Gomer's story with pity or judgment. She is remembered for what she was—a harlot, a woman of the streets, unfaithful. But Scripture never gives us Gomer's voice. She is seen but not heard. Present, but never speaking. We know her actions, but not her pain.

And that silence is familiar.

For generations, African American women have endured life with wounds they could not name, trauma they could not articulate, and pain they were not allowed to process. Like Gomer, many have become defined by what they have done to survive, not by who they truly are.

Gomer's Silence Speaks Volumes

We do not know why Gomer lived the life she did. Was it forced? Was it economic survival? Was it learned behavior from a broken lineage?

We do not know.

And that silence opens the door to reflection. Because silence does not mean absence—it often means suppression.

In today's world, many women carry the Gomer narrative:

Abused in childhood but told, "Don't tell."

Exploited in relationships but advised to "keep the family together."

Degraded at work or in church but expected to "be strong and smile."

The silence that surrounded Gomer still surrounds millions of women. It is the silence of survival.

What Hosea Did Not Know

Survival trains a woman to hustle, to run, to numb. But it does not teach her how to be still in safety.

Gomer had no idea how to be a wife—how to live without being bought, used, or thrown away. She may have felt more comfortable in captivity than in covenant.

Many modern women face this same crisis: When you have built your identity around pain and performance, love feels like a threat, not a gift.

The Past Is Not the Final Chapter

The good news is God saw past Gomer's pain and gave her a prophetic future. Not because of her works— but because of her worth to Him.

Gomer is every woman who has been discarded and yet still has a destiny.

You are not your past.

You are not what they called you.

You are not what you had to do to survive.

Healing the Gomer Within

To heal the Gomer inside, we must:

Create safe spaces for women to speak their truth.

Break the shame that comes with survival.

Teach the difference between love and control.

Provide resources for mental, emotional, and spiritual healing.

The same God who commanded Hosea to love Gomer still loves you today—with that same unwavering, redeeming love.

CHAPTER 14:
HOSEA'S OBEDIENCE – LOVING WHEN IT DOES NOT MAKE SENSE

There are few commands in Scripture more baffling than what God told the prophet Hosea: "Go, marry a promiscuous woman and have children with her..." (Hosea 1:2). To love someone unfaithful, unstable, and unworthy by society's standards is hard enough—but to do it by divine instruction?

That is obedience beyond logic.

In a culture where love is often based on compatibility, appearance, or performance, Hosea's love confronts us with a deeper truth: Sometimes, God asks you to love someone not for what they give you, but for what He is doing through you.

This is a painful, holy, often misunderstood love—and it reflects the heart of God Himself.

Love That Costs Something

Hosea's love cost him his pride. It damaged his reputation. It broke his heart more than once.

But he did not walk away.

This is the kind of love few want to sign up for—but many are called to carry:

Loving a parent who abandoned you.

Standing by a spouse battling addiction or relapse.

Raising children who do not yet understand your sacrifices.

Ministering to a community that mistrusts your intentions.

This kind of love hurts, but it heals, not because of who is being loved, but because of who is doing the loving.

Obedience Without Understanding

Obedience often precedes understanding. Hosea did not know what God was fully up to. He just knew what he was commanded to do.

And that is where many believers—especially African American women—find themselves. Called to love people who do not love them back. Expected to pour out in homes, churches, and systems that take more than they give. Tasked with carrying burdens they did not ask for.

Like Hosea, they love out of obedience, not reciprocity.

God's Heart Revealed Through Hosea

Hosea's marriage was not him and Gomer—it was a prophetic picture of God's love for Israel. His heartbreak mirrored God's heartbreak. His loyalty reflected divine mercy.

Sometimes your personal pain has a public purpose.

Your story might be shaping someone else's healing.

Your obedience might be interceding for a generation.

Your endurance might be unlocking restoration in a bloodline.

Redefining Masculinity and Ministry

In today's culture, Hosea's obedience challenges traditional ideas of masculinity:

He was not passive—he was obedient.

He was not weak—he was faithful under pressure.

He did not love to be praised—he loved to reveal God's heart.

To the modern man, Hosea says: Your strength is not in your control—it is in your ability to cover, endure, and redeem.

To women, his love reminds you: There are men who love like God—who stay when it is hard, who see past your past, and who obey when others flee.

Love as Ministry

Hosea teaches us that love is not always romantic—it is spiritual warfare.

It is staying planted when everything tells you to leave.

It is believing in someone when their actions contradict your hope.

It is trusting that God's command to love is not just about them—it is-it is-it is-it is forming something eternal in you.

CHAPTER 15:
ARE THERE ANY RUTHS TODAY?

When African American women say, "I'm waiting on my Boaz," they are often referencing a man who is kind, respectful, responsible, and ready for commitment. But what made Boaz choose Ruth? Why did her story stand out? And the deeper question we must ask is—are there any Ruths today?

In a society that prizes instant gratification, independence over interdependence, and popularity over character, Ruth's story provides a timeless model of virtue, faith, and feminine strength.

Ruth in Context: The Power of Loyalty and Obedience

Ruth was not an Israelite. She was a Moabite—a foreigner, an outsider, a widow, and barren.

And yet, she chose:

Loyalty over convenience — "Where you go, I will go... your God will be my God." (Ruth 1:16)

Humility over pride — She gleaned in fields as a lowly worker.

Obedience over independence — She followed Naomi's counsel in approaching Boaz.

These were not signs of weakness—they were strength in submission, rooted in trust and hope.

What Made Ruth Stand Out?

Boaz was a man of wealth, influence, and wisdom. He was not easily swayed. So, what made Ruth different from others?

Her Character Was Her Calling Card

Boaz said, "All the people of my town know that you are a woman of noble character." (Ruth 3:11)

Ruth did not chase Boaz—her life spoke for her.

She Honored Elders and Legacy

In honoring Naomi, Ruth also honored Naomi's God, customs, and lineage.

She Was Willing to Work

Ruth was not waiting passively. She worked in the fields with dignity and consistency.

She Positioned Herself with Purpose

When Ruth lay at Boaz's feet, she was not being seductive—she was symbolically asking for covenant, for protection, for a future.

Are There Any Ruths Today?

Yes—though they may not always be recognized:

Single mothers who raise children with faith and integrity.

Women in school or working two jobs, sacrificing now for a better future.

Survivors of abuse who choose healing and wholeness over bitterness.

Daughters of the faith who serve their communities, churches, and families with unwavering grace.

Ruths today may wear jeans instead of robes, speak slang instead of Hebrew, but their hearts are just as noble.

Misconceptions About Being a "Ruth"

Today, some confuse being a Ruth with:

Being passive and waiting endlessly.

Accepting any kind of mistreatment in the name of loyalty.

Losing themselves while trying to earn a Boaz.

But Ruth did not wait idly—she moved in wisdom, timing, and alignment with purpose. She did not chase Boaz—she obeyed God, and Boaz recognized her virtue.

Ruth's Qualities in the 21st Century Woman

If you want to reflect Ruth's spirit today, here are a few timeless qualities to pursue:

Loyalty Without Losing Yourself

Stand with people, but not at the cost of your dignity or destiny.

Humility That Honors God

Know who you are, but also know who God is. Ruth bowed low, not because she was weak, but because she was wise.

Patience with Purpose

Ruth did not rush the process. She let God's timing unfold.

Integrity that Attracts

You do not have to manipulate your way into anyone's heart. Let your life do the talking.

What the World Needs Now: More Ruths

Ruths are the bridge between trauma and triumph, between survival and purpose.

In a world of Gomers struggling to believe they are worthy of love, and Boazes wondering if any women are still willing to be vulnerable without manipulation, Ruths are the balance. They teach us that love is possible after loss, favor follows faithfulness, and purpose is greater than pain.

From Ruth to Revelation

Ruth was not just a love story. It was a destiny story.

She became the great-grandmother of King David, placing her directly in the lineage of Jesus Christ.

This is the power of one woman's loyalty, obedience, and integrity.

If you are a Ruth, or desire to become one, know this:

God sees your quiet sacrifices.

Favor may not be loud, but it will find you.

Your story is not over—your Boaz moment may still be on its way.

CHAPTER 16:
WHEN LOVE DOES NOT FIT THE FORMULA –
HOSEA AND THE DISRUPTION OF
EXPECTATIONS

Black women today are often encouraged to create vision boards for their future—lists of what they want in a man, a career, a lifestyle. Structure. Order. Expectation. But what happens when love does not show up the way you imagined?

What happens when God sends someone into your life who does not check your boxes but challenges your calling?

This was Hosea's story. And for many Black women, it is theirs too.

The Discomfort of Divine Instruction

Hosea did not go looking for Gomer. God sent him to her. It was divine, but it was not pretty. Purposeful, but painful. Hosea had to surrender his expectations of what love should look like to obey a calling that looked like a contradiction.

Many Black women are in the same space: faithful, focused, and prayerful—yet drawn to situations and people that disrupt their expectations. Not because they are wrong, but because God is working something deeper in them.

Sometimes the love story you are given is not about romance—it is about revelation.

When Purpose Feels Like a Problem

Hosea's assignment to love Gomer was not about compatibility. It was about showing how far God was willing to go to show mercy. His life became the message. And for today's Black woman, many find themselves loving in spaces that feel less like dreams and more like burdens.

You may be loving a sibling through mental illness.

Raising a child without support.

Supporting a friend who's lost in identity.

Praying for a partner who is emotionally unavailable.

And you wonder: God, why does this love feel so heavy?

Like Hosea, the weight is not punishment—it is purpose. But that does not mean it is easy.

Letting Go of the Formula

The formula says:

Be perfect.

Date perfect.

Marry perfect.

Live happily ever after.

But Black women have learned that real life rarely honors formulas. Love can be messy. It can come in waves. It can teach through discomfort. And sometimes, the people you are called to love are the ones who reflect the broken parts of you, too.

Hosea teaches us that obedience to God may lead us into places that challenge our pride, our past, and our feelings of love.

Loving Without Losing Yourself

It is important to say this clearly: Loving someone does not mean erasing yourself.

Hosea never stopped being a prophet when he became Gomer's husband. Likewise, a Black woman must never abandon her identity just to hold onto someone else's. Your call, your dignity, and your peace matter, even when you are asked to love sacrificially.

Loving someone who is difficult does not make you holy. Loving them with boundaries and clarity—that's wisdom.

Love and the Desire to Be Loved Back

Many Black women today find themselves questioning: "Why do I keep showing up for people who don't show up for me?" The answer may lie in what you have been taught about your worth.

You deserve love that reflects God's heart—not just His mercy.

Yes, love requires grace. But grace is not the absence of accountability.

Black Women and the Disrupted Love Story

For some Black women, love does not come in the traditional form of husband and wife. Sometimes it looks like:

A life partner who is not male, challenging long-held ideas of love and identity.

A non-romantic covenant friendship that nurtures you more than any relationship ever has.

A single season that is not empty, but full of clarity, growth, and peace.

Love that does not fit the formula is not failed love. It is often the truest form of it.

Hosea's Lesson for the Black Woman

Hosea reminds you that love is not just what you feel—it is what you do. It is what you surrender. It is what you learn when nothing goes according to plan.

And sometimes, God uses love not to give you someone, but to grow you into someone.

Love is not just a feeling that always feels good.

Love does not always respond or act as it should.

Love can be sweet, and it can be kind, but true love is not

Something that you can always find.

Love has levels and conditions that are in our minds.

But the love that is missing comes from God, granted to everyone

From the very start. And the true essence of love is a matter of the heart.

+++The Author

CHAPTER 17:
RUTH REIMAGINED – THE BLACK WOMAN WHO REFUSES TO SETTLE

Ruth's story is often romanticized: a beautiful woman gleans in a field, catches the eye of a wealthy man, and lives happily ever after. But there is more to Ruth than what has been filtered through Sunday School and social media.

Ruth is not just the woman who got Boaz.

She is the woman who refused to go back to what was comfortable.

And today's Black woman is doing the same.

Ruth did not chase a Man—She Chased Purpose.

Ruth's defining moment was not in the barley field—it was in her decision to leave what was familiar and follow Naomi into the unknown. She said, "Where you go, I will go," not because she had a full plan, but because she had full faith.

That is what so many Black women are doing now. Leaving toxic environments. Walking away from halfhearted relationships. Declining job offers that compromise peace. Choosing growth, even if it means walking alone for a season.

Ruth did not wait for Boaz. She moved in integrity.

Boaz did not confirm her worth. He recognized what was already there.

The Power of Not Settling

Refusing to settle is not arrogance—it is alignment.

It is the understanding that God's timing is worth more than emotional convenience.

Today's Black woman is reclaiming her standards—not out of stubbornness, but out of self-respect.

She is no longer:

Lowering her voice to be chosen.

Shrinking her dreams to keep peace.

Saying "yes" when her spirit says "no."

She is embracing her inner Ruth, who waited with dignity while still working in the field.

The Work Before the Reward

Before Ruth met Boaz, she was in the field, in motion. Her character was already in full display: diligent, humble, courageous. Boaz noticed Ruth because Ruth was already becoming who she was called to be.

Black women today are not waiting for a savior. They are:

Building businesses.

Finishing degrees.

Raising families.

Healing generational trauma.

They are not idle—they are intentional.

And if love comes, it must align with their progress, not distract from it.

The Modern Ruth Is Not Desperate

She is open to love but not obsessed with it.

She values partnership, but not at the cost of peace.

She honors companionship, but not without covenant-level commitment.

Ruth reimagined is not afraid of being alone. She is afraid of being misaligned.

And that shift is powerful.

Boaz was not the Goal—He was the Confirmation.

Ruth did not sit around hoping for a man to fix her life. She was already living, already serving, already believing. When Boaz appeared, it was not a rescue—it was a reward.

Boaz did not complete Ruth's story. He became part of it because she was already whole.

Today's Black woman is not waiting for a man to define her future. She is preparing for divine alignment—and trusting that any connection God brings will reflect the quality of the life she is already building.

For the Black Woman Who's Still Waiting

Do not let culture rush you.

Do not let loneliness lie to you.

Do not let trends teach you to compromise.

You are not being overlooked—you are being preserved.

Ruth had no clue that her obedience would make her the great-grandmother of a king. She did not see legacy—she saw one decision at a time.

That is what today's Black woman is doing.

Choosing obedience over convenience.

Choosing clarity over chaos.

Choosing faith over fear.

And that is what makes her powerful.

CHAPTER 18:
GOMER'S DAUGHTERS – THE JOURNEY OF THE BLACK WOMAN STILL LEARNING TO LOVE HERSELF

Gomer's name rarely comes up in messages of hope. She is often treated like a warning, not a woman. But her story—raw, complex, and uncomfortable—echoes in the lives of many Black women today who find themselves caught between longing for love and feeling unworthy of it.

If Ruth represents the woman who moves with intention, Gomer is the woman who is still learning how to stay.

When You Do Not Feel Worthy of Being Chosen

Hosea chose Gomer before she was healed.

Loved before she was ready.

Brought into a home before she knew how to be at peace.

And many Black women today know what it is like to be handed love while still holding shame. To be invited into care while still battling mistrust. To have someone say, "I see you," while you are still trying to recognize yourself in the mirror.

There is nothing easy about being Gomer's daughter.

But there is nothing unworthy about her either.

The Struggle Between Love and Self-Sabotage

For some Black women, when love gets too close, fear gets louder.

Fear of being hurt again.

Fear of not measuring up.

Fear that the past will find a way to ruin the present.

Gomer ran—not because she did not want to be loved, but because she did not know how to be loved and still feel safe.

That fear does not make a woman weak. It makes her human.

Healing Is Not Linear

Today's Black woman who identifies with Gomer may still be unlearning:

That performance is not required for worth.

That emotional availability is not a weakness.

That stability does not have to be followed by betrayal.

That being loved does not mean being controlled.

Healing is not about arriving—it is about returning.

Returning to yourself.

Returning to truth.

Returning to a belief that you are worth staying for.

When You Have Been Chosen But Cannot Receive It.

Hosea stayed. That is a powerful truth. But more powerful is this: God did not ask Gomer to earn Hosea's love—He asked Hosea to extend it.

The message? Love is not always logical, but when it is divine, it is persistent.

Some Black women today are being offered real, patient love—not just from people, but from God Himself—and are still learning how to receive it without apology.

You are not broken because you flinch when kindness comes.

You are healing because you notice it.

Love Must Come with Accountability

Being loved does not mean staying stuck. Hosea did not just rescue Gomer—he bought her back and asked her to return home with a new understanding.

True love holds space, but it also holds standards.

It does not just say, "I'll take you back."

It says, "I'll walk with you as we grow together."

Black women who feel like Gomer do not need pity. They need partnership—the kind that does not abandon them in the dark but also does not let them stay in denial.

The Gomer Identity Is Not Permanent

You may feel like Gomer now—scattered, unsure, or caught in patterns that do not reflect your worth. But Gomer was not always lost.

She had a home.

She had a husband.

She had a new beginning.

The story did not end with shame. It ended with restoration.

And for the Black woman who sees herself in Gomer—your restoration is not a fantasy, it is a process. And it is not too late.

Today's Gomer: Healing in Real Time

Today's Gomer is going to therapy.

She is reclaiming her voice.

She is setting new boundaries.

She is learning to receive love without suspicion.

And in some cases, she is learning to love herself first before asking anyone else to.

She may still stumble, but she stands up faster.

She may still question her worth, but she does not walk away from it.

She may still be growing—but she is growing.

And that alone makes her worthy of every good thing coming.

CHAPTER 19:
WHEN BLACK WOMEN LOVE EACH OTHER – SISTERHOOD, SUPPORT, AND SACRED SPACE

We talk a lot about romantic love. But some of the most transformative, soul-stretching love comes not from a man, but from another Black woman—through the power of sisterhood.

In a world that too often pits women against one another or tells them that love must look romantic to be real, today's Black woman is reclaiming the sacredness of connection. Real, soul-deep, no-performance-required connection.

Boaz and Hosea showed us love in the context of romantic pursuit.

But what happens when healing comes from each other?

Sisterhood That Heals

Today's Black woman is building communities where she can:

Cry without shame

Speak without censor

Heal without judgment

Grow without fear

These relationships are not just "friendships"—they are lifelines.

Many of the burdens Black women carry are not lightened in therapy or church alone—they are eased in the laughter, late-night phone calls, and unspoken understanding of another woman who gets it.

This is more than community.

It is communion.

The Love That Does Not Have to Be Explained

There are Black women forming bonds so deep that others mistake them for something romantic. And sometimes, that is true, too. Sometimes what begins as sisterhood blossoms into something more, and rather than deny that possibility, many Black women are learning to explore the fluidity of love without shame.

But whether platonic or romantic, there is a power in woman-to-woman love that affirms identity. A love that says:

"You don't have to be strong here."

"I see you when the world overlooks you."

"You're not too much, and you're not not enough."

That is a love that heals.

When You Have Been Hurt by Other Women

Let us be honest, sisterhood is not always easy.

Some of the deepest wounds carried by Black women have come from other Black women.

Competition. Betrayal. Silence when protection was needed.

But healing does not come by avoiding connection. It comes by redefining it.

It takes courage to say:

"I've been hurt by women, but I still believe in the power of women."

"I've seen pettiness, but I've also seen compassion."

"I've experienced gossip, but I've also experienced grace."

That balance is holy.

Sisterhood as Sacred Ground

In Ruth's story, before there was Boaz, there was Naomi.

It was her loyalty to Naomi that set the whole love story in motion.

We often overlook that. But in many Black women's lives today, their Naomi came before their Boaz. A woman who mentored, mothered, or walked with them through valleys they could not have survived alone.

Whether it is a biological sister, a best friend, a church mother, or a chosen family member—these sacred bonds are more than supportive. They are spiritual.

They keep us alive.

The Beauty of Black Women Choosing Each Other

We are seeing more Black women celebrate each other loudly.

Lifting as they climb.

Celebrating without competition.

Correcting with love, not shame.

It is a revolution of softness. A resistance to isolation. A restoration of trust.

And for some, it is the first place where they have experienced safe love—not for how they look, or what they give, but for who they are.

If You've Lost Faith in Sisterhood...

Let this be your reminder: There are still Black women who will love you purely.

They will show up for you without jealousy.

They will speak life into you without strings.

They will challenge you without shaming you.

They will stand beside you when others walk away.

Love does not only flow vertically—from man to woman. It flows laterally—from woman to woman, and it can be just as divine, just as restorative, just as real.

CHAPTER 20:
THE POWER OF CHOOSING BOAZ ENERGY – WHEN THE BLACK WOMAN STOPS CHASING AND STARTS ATTRACTING

There comes a moment in a Black woman's life when she stops asking, "When will he choose me?" and starts asking, "Am I choosing peace, wholeness, and alignment?"

Boaz did not show up because Ruth begged, chased, or pleaded.

He noticed her because she was doing what she was called to do.

That is what "Boaz energy" is: it is attraction through alignment.

Boaz Energy Is Not Just About the Man

Let us be clear—Boaz is more than a romantic partner.

He is in favor, stability, integrity, and intentionality.

So, when a Black woman decides, she is done chasing broken promises, old habits, and emotionally unavailable people—she does not just attract a "man like Boaz," she attracts:

Healthier relationships

Elevated opportunities

Friendships that feed her soul

Peace that money cannot buy

Choosing Boaz energy means choosing yourself differently.

Chasing Is Exhausting, But Attracting Is Empowering

Black women have been taught for generations that they have to do the most just to get a little in return. Be loud enough to be seen. Be soft enough to be palatable. Be loyal even when it hurts.

But when she chooses Boaz Energy, the script flips.

She is no longer:

Trying to convince someone of her worth.

Shrinking her identity to be more "dateable."

Waiting for a text to validate her day.

Instead, she stands in full authority and says,

"If it's not aligned with my peace, it's not for me."

The Power of Presence Over Performance

Boaz noticed Ruth because of her presence, not performance.

She was working in the field, minding her business, and living with quiet dignity.

Today's Black woman is learning the same principle.

She is no longer in a race to be chosen.

She is choosing herself daily—and that glow is magnetic.

Peace attracts what desperation repels.

Clarity attracts what confusion complicates.

Purpose attracts what chaos delays.

That is the shift.

The Difference Between Being Pursued and Being Played

There is a real difference between being pursued with purpose and being played with for entertainment.

Boaz did not confuse Ruth. He did not breadcrumb her. He did not string her along.

He saw her. Respected her. Moved intentionally toward her.

Black women today are reclaiming the right to expect clarity.

They are done with mixed signals.

They are done with emotional manipulation.

They are done with guessing games.

Boaz energy demands honesty and consistency—not potential and excuses.

You Are the Prize, Not the Pawn

Boaz did not rescue Ruth. He recognized her.

He did not say, "Let me save you."

He said, "You've already proven who you are."

That is what happens when a Black woman walks into Boaz Energy.

She does not wait to be crowned—she walks like royalty before anyone acknowledges it.

She does not beg.

She does not bend for validation.

She does not build someone hoping they will build her back.

She honors herself, and that honor becomes a magnet for what matches.

What Boaz Energy Looks Like in Today's Black Woman

She is no longer chasing hustle. She is embracing balance.

She is no longer trying to "fix" people. She is focused on her growth.

She is no longer tolerating chaos. She is cultivating clarity.

She is no longer playing small. She owns her greatness.

This is not arrogance. It is awareness.

It is not an attitude. It is alignment.

It is not intimidation. It is identity.

And when she moves like that—Boaz does not just show up...

He stays.

CHAPTER 21:
WHAT HOSEA TEACHES US ABOUT LOVING WITHOUT LOSING YOURSELF

Hosea's love was powerful. Painful. Prophetic.

But it raises a question many Black women are asking today:

How do you love deeply without disappearing in the process?

Hosea was commanded to marry Gomer, a woman who would betray his love multiple times. Yet he stayed, loved, pursued, and even redeemed her. His story reflects a divine, selfless love—but not a blueprint for self-erasure.

The Beauty and the Burden of Unconditional Love

Loving like Hosea can feel holy—but it can also feel heavy.

Some Black women have found themselves in Hosea-shaped roles:

Loving men who were emotionally unavailable.

Rescuing people who never intended to change.

Pouring into others with nothing poured back into them.

It is time to say this clearly:

Unconditional love is powerful, but it should not come at the cost of your peace, purpose, or personal identity.

Hosea loved as an act of divine obedience, not personal codependency.

You Are Not God to Anyone

Many Black women have been socialized to believe that love means endurance—that if you just pray harder, stay longer, love deeper, the person will change.

But you are not God.

You are not someone's redemption story.

You are not the sacrifice they need to get better.

That was Hosea's divine assignment.

It does not need to be yours.

Love can be holy without being harmful.

Love Should Not Leave You Empty

Hosea did not chase Gomer out of desperation—he returned for her out of covenant. He was aligned with God's will.

Today's Black woman must ask:

Am I staying because I am anointed to, or am I afraid of starting over?

Am I loving them into healing, or losing myself in their dysfunction?

Godly love does not require you to erase yourself to be effective.

You can love someone and still say:

"I need space."

"I deserve honesty."

"I can't keep carrying both of us."

Boundaries are not betrayal—they are survival.

What Loving Without Losing Yourself Looks Like

It means checking in with your own emotional health as often as you check on theirs.

It means walking away if the relationship becomes a cycle instead of a covenant.

It means choosing peace over potential.

It means saying: "I can love you and still leave."

Loving someone with Hosea's heart does not mean becoming Gomer's prison.

It means showing compassion without giving up your own liberation.

Not Everyone Is Your Assignment

Hosea's love was a prophetic act—symbolic of God's relationship with Israel. It was never meant to be a universal relationship model.

Many Black women today carry the weight of "saving" their partners, families, or friends. But some of the people you are fighting to rescue were never yours to redeem.

Let this be a release:

You do not have to be Hosea in every relationship.

Sometimes love looks like letting go.

Sometimes rescue looks like refusing to be the rescuer.

A Better Kind of Love Is Possible

Hosea's story reminds us that love requires grace—but it also demands discernment.

You can:

Love them.

Forgive them.

Pray for them.

But still choose yourself.

Because when you stop losing yourself to love others, you will finally discover what it feels like to be loved without condition and without compromise.

CHAPTER 22:
GOD KNOWS HER NAME – WHEN THE BLACK WOMAN FEELS FORGOTTEN

There is a sacred ache many Black women carry.

Not the loud kind.

The silent kind.

The kind that says:

"I'm strong for everyone else, but who's strong for me?"

"I'm celebrated publicly, but invisible privately."

"I pour out daily, but does anyone know what I really need?"

This chapter is for her. The Black woman who shows up with a full face and an empty heart. The woman who wonders if anyone—including God—truly sees her.

Let us begin here: God knows your name.

The World Might Overlook You, But Heaven Does Not

Ruth was a Moabite. An outsider. A woman from the margins.

Yet God wove her into the lineage of Christ.

Gomer was labeled, judged, and discarded.

Yet God used her story to reveal His mercy and grace.

Repeatedly, God uses the overlooked to show His care.

And that has not changed.

Today's Black woman may not always be acknowledged by systems, institutions, or even the people closest to her. But there is a God who:

Sees the unseen moments.

Keeps the whispered prayers.

Records the tears nobody else even noticed.

You are not forgotten.

When No One Checks on You, God Covers You

Many Black women are pillars in their homes, churches, and communities.

But even pillars crack when the weight becomes too much.

And while the world applauds your strength, you may be screaming inside:

"Who checks on me?"

"Why do I always have to be the strong one?"

"When is it my turn to rest?"

Hear this clearly: Even when no one checks on you, God covers you.

He is the whisper in the quiet.

The stillness in the storm.

The hand that catches what you do not even have words to pray for.

You Are More Than What You Do

Sometimes the pain of feeling forgotten comes from being valued only for what you produce, not who you are.

But God does not love you because of what you do.

He loves you because of who you are.

And He knows your name—not just your roles.

He sees the woman, not just the mother.

He sees the soul, not just the title.

He sees the need, not just the strength.

This is personal.

When You Feel Passed Over, Remember Ruth

Ruth did not chase favor. She walked in faith.

She kept showing up—in grief, in humility, in service.

And God sent favor to find her.

If you have been feeling passed over—professionally, emotionally, relationally—remember:

God's favor is not limited by man's recognition.

Sometimes the delay is not a rejection.

It is redirection.

And just because they do not see you does not mean God forgot you.

From Forgotten to Favored

You may not be the loudest voice in the room.

You may not be the one they pick first.

You may not even have the support you need.

But you have a God who majors in divine reversals.

He took Ruth from gleaning to ownership.

He took Gomer from shame to redemption.

He can take you from overlooked to overflowing.

Because heaven does not lose track of the ones this world forgets.

CHAPTER 23:
GOMER'S GRANDDAUGHTERS – THE REDEMPTION STORY OF TODAY'S BLACK WOMAN

Gomer's name is rarely mentioned in sermons without being followed by shame.

But her story is not one of defeat—it is one of redemption.

She was a woman with a past, yes. But she was also a woman with a purpose.

She was pursued, rescued, and reclaimed—not because she was perfect, but because God had a point to make:

Your history does not cancel your destiny.

And now, generations later, her spiritual daughters walk among us.

They are the Gomer granddaughters—Black women who know pain, who know being misunderstood, and who long for a kind of love that does not punish them for their past.

She's Not Just a Statistic—She is a Story

Today's Black woman often lives with contradictions.

She is educated but still judged by her appearance.

She is nurturing but labeled aggressive when she advocates for herself.

She is expressive but criticized for being "too much."

And for those who have had complex journeys—through heartbreak, rejection, cycles of inconsistent love, or even same-sex attractions—society has been quick to define them by labels instead of letting them live their stories.

But Gomer's story teaches us this:

You are more than the worst thing you have been through.

Love That Redeems, Not Condemns

The love Hosea offered Gomer was radical. It did not ignore her flaws, but it also did not define her by them.

Today's Black woman does not need a partner who will "fix" her—she needs someone who will see her, choose her, and walk beside her through transformation. She wants connection, not correction.

Even those navigating the complexity of same-gender desires or identity conflicts still yearn for the same things:

To be loved fully, not conditionally.

To be seen beyond performance.

To be held without having to explain every wound.

God's love, like Hosea's, stretches beyond societal rules—it reaches into the deep and still calls her Beloved.

She's Still Worth Coming After

One of the most powerful moments in Hosea's story is when he goes after Gomer—after her betrayal, after her shame, after she is sold into bondage.

He does not just forgive her. He fights for her.

That kind of pursuit is not just biblical—it is prophetic.

And it still happens today.

Today's Black woman deserves to know that even if she has been through things she does not speak about, even if she has made decisions she is not proud of, she is still worth pursuing, protecting, and loving.

Not because she is perfect. But because she is still God's daughter.

Gomer's Granddaughters Are Rising

They are the ones who:

Choose therapy and healing over silence.

Set boundaries where there used to be brokenness.

Refuse to let shame write the last chapter.

They are the ones learning to receive love again—on their terms, at their pace, in their wholeness.

They are not waiting for society's permission to rise.

They are rising anyway.

And like Gomer, they will not be remembered for where they started. They will be known for how they survived, how they evolved, and how God never gave up on them.

CHAPTER 24:
BOAZ AND HOSEA – A STUDY IN CONTRAST, A REVELATION OF LOVE

For years, many Black women have declared, "I'm waiting on my Boaz," with hope, faith, and a longing for security, stability, and God-ordained love. But few ever say, "I'm waiting on my Hosea."

Why?

God chose men.

Both showed radical love.

Both are married women with broken and uncertain pasts.

Yet the difference lies in the kind of assignment each man carried, and the kind of journey each love story needed.

This concluding chapter will lay bare the distinctions between Boaz and Hosea—two men, two missions, one God.

Boaz: A Man of Provision, Peace, and Preservation

Boaz was a landowner, a man of integrity, wealth, and social standing.

He did not chase drama—he moved with purpose and order.

His love for Ruth came:

After seeing her loyalty.

After watching her consistency.

After witnessing her integrity in obscurity.

Boaz did not see Ruth as a problem to fix.

He saw her as a partner worthy of protection and legacy.

When today's Black woman says she is waiting on her "Boaz,"

What she often says is:

"I want a man who sees me whole—not broken.

I want peace after pain.

I want to be chosen for who I am, not rescued from what I was."

Boaz is the love that honors your healing.

Hosea: A Man of Sacrifice, Suffering, and Unrelenting Obedience

Hosea was a prophet—faithful, obedient, and deeply spiritual.

But his love story was not born out of desire. It was born out of divine instruction.

God told him to marry Gomer, a woman whose behavior would break his heart.

Not once. Not twice. But repeatedly.

Hosea did not just marry Gomer—he redeemed her.

He loved through betrayal.

He restored what others discarded.

He represented God's grace in the face of spiritual adultery.

The Hosea kind of love is not romantic in the traditional sense.

It is costly. Painful. Purposeful.

When today's Black woman looks at Hosea's story, she may say:

> "I do not want to be tolerated. I want to be treasured. I do not want to be someone's assignment. I want to be their desire."

Hosea is the love that enters your chaos but stays anyway.

Assignment vs. Affection

Boaz married Ruth out of mutual honor.

Hosea married Gomer out of divine assignment.

Boaz's story feels like a reward.

Hosea's story feels like a burden.

Boaz chose Ruth after watching her character unfold.

Hosea was commanded to love a woman whose instability brought shame and pain.

This difference matters.

Because many Black women today are tired of being projects.

They want a love story that starts in peace, not pity.

They do not want to be someone's burden or lesson—they want to be someone's blessing.

The Black Woman's Cry: Not Just to Be Loved, But to Be Safe

In this cultural moment, Black women are asking deeper questions:

Can I be loved without having to be fixed?

Can I be honored without having to prove myself?

Can someone choose me not because God told them to, but because they want me?

Boaz reflects the kind of love that meets a healed heart.

Hosea reflects the kind of love that loves through wreckage.

Both are biblical.

Both are powerful.

But the journey is different.

Boaz or Hosea: What Kind of Love Are You Truly Ready For?

Some women carry Gomer's past, but long for Boaz's peace.

Others carry Ruth's faithfulness but find themselves in Hosea-style relationships—fighting to be seen, constantly redeemed, emotionally bruised.

This is why understanding the difference matters.

Because one love affirms what is already restored.

The other love survives what is constantly breaking.

Neither man is "better."

Both were obedient. Both were faithful.

But the question is: What season are you in?

Are you ready for love that affirms your growth like Boaz?

Or are you still healing, needing mercy, like Gomer with Hosea?

God uses both types of men to reveal His heart.

But wisdom helps you discern what your soul truly needs.

Final Thought: Redemption or Reward?

Hosea's love was redemptive.

Boaz's love was rewarding.

Some women feel they have had enough suffering in life—they are not looking for redemption, they are ready for reward.

Others are still mending—still finding their way back—and need someone who loves like Hosea: patiently, prophetically, purposefully.

Wherever you are, know this:

God has not forgotten how to send the right one.

But more importantly, He has not stopped loving you himself.

Conclusion: The Truth We Have Been Waiting For

She is not waiting for a fairy tale.

She is not waiting to be rescued.

She is waiting to be seen.

Not for what she has done, or where she has been—but for who she is becoming.

For generations, Black women have carried the question quietly in their hearts:

"Will anyone ever love me whole?"

Some have searched for a Boaz—a man who recognizes their worth after the storm.

Others have survived relationships that felt more like Hosea—loving through brokenness, shame, and a fight to reclaim identity.

But what if this was never about the man?

What if it was about the message?

Whether you are like Ruth—disciplined, faithful, humble...

Or like Gomer—flawed, misunderstood, and aching to be restored...

You are still worthy of love.

You are still in the story.

The Mirror We Needed

Boaz and Hosea are not just characters.

They are mirrors. Boaz reflects the man who loves a healed woman.

Hosea reflects the man who stays when healing has not yet begun.

But deeper still, they both reflect God.

A God who:

Honors loyalty like Boaz.

Pursues the broken like Hosea.

Covers shame like Boaz.

Redeems bondage like Hosea.

Chooses repeatedly, even when others walk away.

That is the kind of love today's Black woman needs.

And that is the kind of love she already has—in God.

The Woman in the Middle

This book was never about the men.

It was about the woman in the middle—you.

The Black woman who has endured, survived, led, prayed, rebuilt, raised generations, worked twice as hard for half the credit, and still held her head high.

The Black woman who may have been Ruth in one season, Gomer in another, and Naomi somewhere in between.

This is your reminder:

You do not have to wait to be loved.

You already are.

You do not have to chase Boaz.

You do not have to fear Hosea.

Because the same God who used both men for His glory is authoring your story too.

From Survival to Significance

You are not just surviving.

You are shifting generations.

You are not just healing.

You are becoming whole.

You are not waiting for love to show up at your door.

You are walking in love every day—with your decisions, your discipline, your growth, and your grace.

Whether your path looks like Ruth's harvest or Gomer's redemption,

God is not finished.

There is still a love out there that will:

Celebrate your strength.

Hold space for your softness.

Respect your boundaries.

Desire your presence.

And honor your becoming.

Final Declaration

So let this book end with a declaration—not of desperation, but of destiny:

I am not waiting for Boaz.

I am not reliving Hosea.

I am becoming the woman God already loves.

And love, real love, will find me in my wholeness.

You are not forgotten.

You are not invisible.

You are not too far gone.

You are not too late.

You are the difference.

You are the legacy.

You are the Ruth and the redemption.

You are the Gomer and the glory.

And this—this love story?

It is just getting started.

www.ingramcontent.com/pod-product-compliance
Lightning Source LLC
Chambersburg PA
CBHW040845120626
46547CB00001B/38